CONTENTS

THE RENT EATS FIRST

WHEN A REAL ADULT WALKS INTO MY OFFICE SEEKING LEGAL ADVICE

eyes swelling like a housing bubble
and before i can
even introduce myself asks

What should I do? The bank is trying
to take my house. I have a family. I have no way
to pay. What should I do?

i should have something
useful to say. i'm a lawyer.
but all i can think of is

my studio apartment
carpeted with dirty laundry
my yahoo account

how i blush when i buy condoms
i'm not sure if my socks are clean
my beard is bad taxidermy
my tv has a vhs player
none of my clocks are set correctly
this morning i had to wait to shower
so the bathwater could drain
from the night before, and
eight days ago i took the
wrong bus

and this man
is seeking advice
from me

this man with a home
and a family,
and ironed pants

...AFTER A SMALL VICTORY IN A MIDWEST COURTHOUSE

In these parts of the state, you do not Karl Marx someone's home back. You Adam Smith it. You handshake. Glad-hand. Hand job. Bleed. You bleed it back. You do not photojournalist bleed. You do not dead crow sidewalk metaphor bleed. You throat bleed. So deep in the throat you don't know it's blood. Don't spit blood. You'll stain the rug.

Say thank you. *thank you, Your Honor thank you of course you're right thank you thank you thank you thank you if it pleases the Court thank you if i may, Your Honor thank you i'm sorry, Your Honor thank you just one last point, Your Honor thank you thank you thank you thank you if i may, Your Honor*

No, Your Honor. I must have misspoken. That's very funny, Your Honor. Of course he has bootstraps. Of course he doesn't expect to get things for free.

GETTING A PHONE CALL FROM A CLIENT AFTER A FIGHT WITH MY GIRLFRIEND

an anxious pantoum

the office thermostat is stuck at 76 again and the phone is ringing through the computer and the voice on the other end sounds like how men cry when we think we're not actually crying but the number is familiar and i know what's next: "The landlord said they smelled weed outside my place and now I have to leave by Thursday or they'll evict me and my credit will become another fucking ankle bracelet"

I can solve any problem if I think hard enough.

research "drug laws in public housing" if i email the landlord will he roll over? is he even allowed to? sometimes you've gotta really massage a conversation like a sore foot other times it's a knot in the back and you've gotta just kinda start punching

my therapist calls the racing thoughts a symptom but i swear they're a tool, too. the only difference between a sword and a plowshare is what you're cutting

I can solve any problem if I think hard enough.

and then some stupid love song alerts me to a text message *love me love me say that you love me* and i know what's coming jesus, why can't you ever let things go and i know she's right but the bother just keeps dancing up there (*eric, you're being so dumb*) and i know she was kidding and we talked about it but "it wasn't what you said just how you said it" not like a joke like something else but i've already said that twice already so i just listen to my phone sing *love me love me say that you love me* for like thirty seconds and then i'm back to this email to the landlord

My therapist calls the racing thoughts a symptom but I swear they're a tool, too.

i just want pills that work at home and not at the office so my thoughts only barb wire the slumlords not the people who try to get close to me because now there's this unread text message just sitting there festering until i write back can we talk and thirty second later it's *love me love me say that you love me* and i know what's coming of course we can talk but the bother just keeps dancing up there (*eric, you're being so dumb*) and i know she was kidding and we talked about it but "it wasn't what you said, just how you said it" not like a joke like something else but i've already said that twice already so i just listen to my phone sing *love me love me say that you love me* for like thirty seconds and then i'm back to this email to the landlord

see i don't wanna read the phone because sometimes my thoughts are
a scary movie i have to watch through my hands
so now i'm stuck on a word in the email: if this problem is not solved
soon or if this problem is not solved urgently?

urgently it is.

i just want pills that work at home and not at the office so my
thoughts only barbwire the slumlords not the people who try to get
close to me but there's still this unread text message just sitting there
festering *love me love me say that you love me*

and i don't wanna check the phone because sometimes my thoughts
are a scary movie i have to watch through my hands
but my shrink calls that *exposure therapy* so i read well when do you
want to get this solved and move on and i start to write back
obviously i'd like to get it solved
but now i'm stuck on a word soon or urgently? soon or
urgently?

I can solve any problem if I think hard enough.

urgently it is.

[WRITTEN IN REAL-TIME]

My friend Meghan is sitting next to me at the bar.
My friend Meghan's friend Lauren is sitting next to her.
Meghan and I are talking about wealth redistribution
or something. Lauren, on the other hand, is wasted.

At first she was only like Robert-Downey-Jr.-wasted
but now she's more like Lou-Reed-wasted.
When Lauren was only like Piano-Man-wasted
she thought I was pretty funny.

But now that she's like Sweet-Caroline-wasted
she does not like me anymore. I know because
she keeps telling me. For example, she just said

Eric, I do not like you anymore. I do not like you
because of the things you say.

And I tell her I feel the same way and she gets insulted
because she doesn't realize I'm talking about myself
so she calls me an asshole.

Which is fair. I did just come out against polar bears
in an argument. I'm not saying we shouldn't try
to save them but they are mean and will eat us.

In the time it takes my mind to wander back
from my ambivalent feelings about polar bears,
Lauren has crowded me out of the conversation
completely, pointing at me 3 times in 45 seconds, saying

This guy. Not a fan.

So now I am entirely focused on eavesdropping
on the couple three stools to my left

who either just broke up or just met.
But then I hear Lauren talking

about wanting to kill herself or Macklemore
winning a Grammy or something depressing like that

and we make eye contact briefly and it's the type
that scares me because I can suddenly see
so much of myself in someone who was just talking
about death like a friend. But the moment breaks
when Lauren looks at me and mouths

This fuckin' guy.

And now I am back to making eye contact with no one,
eavesdropping on one conversation per ear. I try not to pay
too much attention to Lauren because she is exhausted by life
and if I look at her again I may never look away,
because how can someone as myopic as I am turn away
from introspection disguised as a stranger?

But now the couple to my left are just sitting there
like idling trains, so I decide to look nowhere
and it is Halloween and that I am a broken
periscope.

Again. But then I hear Lauren talking
about scar tissue and I don't know
if she means the Red Hot Chili Peppers' song
or the type of skin that grows when you get singed so deep
that normal skin won't cut it and UV rays can't get passed the scabs
but doctors say it's part of healing.

[REDACTION OF] AN ABANDONMENT NOTICE ON A FORECLOSED HOME

EXHIBIT 1

IMPORTANT!

We found this property to be vacant/abandoned. This information will be reported to the mortgage holder. The mortgage holder has the right and duty to protect this property. The property will be rekeyed and/or winterized within 3 days. If this property is **NOT VACANT**, please contact Safeguard Properties at **877-340-8482.**

SP029

SPI-009/1-10

IMPORTANT!

protect this property.

SP029

SPI-009/1-10

THE FORECLOSURE CRISIS, EXPLAINED THROUGH THE FIRST 80 MINUTES OF DISNEY'S *THE LION KING*

Everything the light touches used to be ours.
Now, foreclosure signs turn our neighborhoods
into metaphors.

First, the loan sharks pull the last solid pieces of meat
from these warm bodies we once called home.
Then the hyenas slink through this elephant graveyard

to pick at the bones. They don't prefer the term
hyenas anymore. Call them *debt collectors.* Call them
board-up companies. Call it the *circle of life.* A food chain is still

a food chain. We all know what to call those
who lap up the blood and sniff out the scrap. We all know the funeral
in store for the prey, the parking lot headstone, the cleansing dirge

of the wrecking ball. There is no Mufasa in this territory,
no noble king, only nominal royalty passing remains down to Scar
until there are too many bones to lick clean. He builds a palace

with the surplus, calls it *the economy,*
hates the term *ghost town,*
prefers the term *marketplace.*

He lays on his throw rug, admires the hair
still on the scalps, mews at the scent
of dried calcium.

[THEY] DON'T REALLY CARE IF YOU CRY

after Lil Uzi Vert

On SoundCloud, in between songs by popular artists
there is a public service announcement urging listeners
against the use of chewing tobacco

because everybody knows those most likely to listen to SoundCloud
are baseball players from the 1930s and sailors
in the World War II Navy.

For example, my grandpa, a veteran himself, would always say to me, *Tatala, it could get so lonely in the Pacific. Thank God I had Lil Yachty there to keep me company.*

According to these commercials, if you chew tobacco, you will lose
your jaw, which is a strange thing to picture
every 1:30 seconds.

But I guess this is the good part of capitalism — using paid advertising
to convince Playboi Carti fans not to chew
their faces into ancient skulls.

I am listening to SoundCloud in my office
because I am a Legal Aid
housing lawyer.

This is the fun part of capitalism — getting paid
to serve righteous vengeance
in a briefcase.

Mortgage banks are the bad part of capitalism.
They're the first to buy flood insurance
on cities they build underwater.

But that's the American dream, ain't it? Having the right stake
in everyone else's fire sale, like Big Tobacco avoiding prosecution
by agreeing to sponsor their own anti-smoking ads.

Studies indicate that any mention of cigarettes
prompts smokers to crave a cigarette. So really, these advertisements
are just ensuring that Depression-era farmer

bumping Lil Uzi Vert enjoys his jaw while it lasts. In other words,
no matter who they're fucking, big business always cums first
but at least the consumer gets the post-coital cigarette

*I don't really care if you cryyyyyyyy*YoU'LL CHEW YOuR JAW oFF

*Push me to the edge*YOu'LL CHEw yOUR JAw OfF yOu'Ll ChEW YOuR jAW oFf yOu'LL shoOt yoUr eYe OuT

*All my friends are dead*You'll siphon the American dr**E**am str**A**ight into your vein un**T**il you become a piece of real es**T**ate and beg the ric**H** to buy you You'll googl**E** yourself until your sea**R**ch h**I**story be**C**omes your only songbook and t**He** o**N**ly ones wh**O** can work and feel things at work out loud are these kids on the internet who can't really rap and can't really sing but can chew their **M**ouths into the kind of robot we ca**N**'t help but foll**O**w because it's just the right genre of e**M**pty

CONTRAPUNTAL OF THE CHRISTIAN NATIONALIST (OR THE JURISPRUDENCE OF JUSTICE AMY CONEY BARRETT)

In the Year of Our Lord
1776
we invented America/
our sins/
no longer sacrilege but rather
God's will,
manifest

Christ returned and
we were forgiven/
our transgressions
erased by

destiny,
a now-invisible blood
of the martyr

on the hands
of patriots
clutching the flag
we carry into battle/
Washington
He crossed the Delaware
The emblem of empire
waving behind him

draped on the cross/

He walked on water. The Christ
as portrayed in so many paintings.

The colors of a new order,
of the type of violence
that makes a man a messiah.

The red. The blue.
The White.

REDACTION/ERASURE OF THE "EPIC OF AMERICA" (THE FIRST TEXT TO USE THE PHRASE *AMERICAN DREAM*)

the United States
is
His own ancestor/
his
birth
in lands other than his own/

being an American
is
the whole colorful pageant of
history
and that American dream
is the greatest
lie
on parchment/
a
Cowboy Song

to

White Folk
for those

in-debted to

the Atlantic

...AFTER A LOSS IN A MIDWEST COURTHOUSE

The problem with law
is that it's made of words,
and the problem with words
is that they make everything dull,
though the bluntest blades
are especially brutal.

The weapons we most fear
are those best camouflaged —
see, e.g., sniper rifle, dirty bomb,
or in the courtroom, the term
for "eviction" draped in its
Latin roots. The casual banter
between expensive men. How the sheriff
maintains calm by simply saying
please and never actually gesturing

to the revolver he keeps loaded
and strapped to his hip,
should some ousted body grow so angry
she's losing her home
that the market's visible hands
decide the only address left
is her own stone-carved name.

There's no crying in court. Every desperate
eye is a man-made desert. Cursing the judge
who just took your home away is a jailable
offense. Lying is the worst offense of all.
Though the oath for witnesses doesn't mention G-d

anymore, you can tell He's still in the room
and that His politics haven't changed much.
Maybe that fear is what keeps the courtroom

calm. How the judge reaps rented land
with the most violent plowshare.
How the sheriff loads his pleasantries
with bullets. Our sterile legalisms and their boring
blades. Our Founding Documents and the chain-linked hands
that forged their parchment.

The US Supreme Court is obsessed
with the Magna Carta, habitually citing
the 13th Century British legal document
as a positive influence over American law,
which seems in poor taste, not only because
it excludes Jews, Muslims, and women
from its protections, but also because it established
the exact legal system our founders revolted against.
Then again, as a matter of craft, the document is
perfect, and what's a little historical erasure
in the face of such gorgeous calligraphy
drafted in deep purple-blue ink
(that looks nothing like blood
once it's left the body)?

Today, I'm representing a veteran
facing eviction in the heart
of the Midwest, which means
all the judges sound like their moms
were Frances McDormand in *Fargo*.
And this is how dull knives become
seen as safe.

Instead of snarling

It's 14 degrees
and your family will be out
on the street,

the judge is soft-spoken, courteous, and encouraging

Oh ya. I'm real sorry, Miss,
but you're gonna have to find a place to live. I'm sure
it'll be ok though. You'll just bundle right up and go
somewhere new

And a look comes over her like she knows
she'll have to triage her own family.
But the only thing left to say is
Your Honor,
Thank you.

CONSTRUCTIVE FEEDBACK FOR SUPREME COURT JUSTICE SAMUEL ALITO

1. You're not the smartest
guy in the room.
You're the dumbest
incel on the Reddit thread.

2. Overturning *Roe*
isn't like overturning *Plessy*.
It's like overturning *Brown*.

3. Abolition.
Integration.
Immigration.
Same-sex marriage.

How will they come for you next?

4. Your claim to colorblindness saddens me,
how each morning you must wake
to another gray sunrise.

5. You write "Are we to believe that... hundreds of [19th Century]
legislators acted out of contempt for Catholics and women?"
as if the question can exist as anything but satire. Perhaps a
more tepid version of earlier drafts:

Are we to believe marital rape
wasn't "rape" at all until
our nation's bicentennial?

Are we to believe we bundled and sold humans
the way we bundle and sell mortgages?

Are we to believe our Founding Fathers
could not distinguish mortar from blood?

6. The question: "who gets to decide
a woman's control of her body —
the woman or the government?"

   Your answer: 13th Century Cleric and
legal scholar, Henry de Bracton.

7. What's frightening about your brand of Christian
is that you believe pure motives make virtue
and you always believe your motives pure.

8. The thoughts, feelings, hopes, and yearnings
of an 18-week-old fetus:

9. Nazi courts were comprised of Germany's greatest legal minds. When crafting decisions, they engaged in vigorous debate and precise analytical reasoning to answer a question like "per statute, is defendant a 'Jew?'"

I'm not saying you're a Nazi. I'm just saying you both pride yourselves on sticking closely to the text.

ON HELPING A NEO-NAZI SAVE HIS HOME

He asks for my help,
his arms covered in hate crimes and scabs.
Jesus says to love your enemies

but what's the fun in that? My G-d takes a different tact. Says
Vengeance. Justice. Flood. Blood. Plague. Salt. Axe. Love

is a victor's narrative. I click my pen like a switchblade. My G-d
has smote men for less. He says he tried to talk to the bank.
That he has nowhere to go. His face softens like a synagogue

turned ember. This man does not know me. Knows my name
but not the seas it's traveled. Else he'd call me the banker.
Tell his friends he'd rather lose his home than accept help
from some "Jew lawyer." He is pleasant

in the way Republicans sometimes are.
Appears humble, but so did the ram replacing Isaac
on the stone. My G-d makes his dessert clear.
Rope. Locust. Stone. Tooth.

My G-d has a point.
But we have outargued G-d before
So in this Midrash

Abraham stays his own hand.
Our grief never grows
fangs.

We form a covenant. Not based on love
but on the mitzvah of tearing down kings.

Even when they are gods. Even when we are kings.
Even when they come for this man
whose home bears such ugly flags.

IT'S MY JOB TO FIX THINGS.

I am funny. In other words, I am observant
and also very sad. But it's good for a punchline.
And maybe that's enough for me.
I don't need other people.

I just want to be the kind of guy who seems likable
in a movie. The sort of person loved
by history more than themselves:
Vincent van Gogh. Herman Melville. Jesus,

I'm trying to get better. I keep reading
about mindfulness, which is I guess what happens
when a ghost possesses its own body. It's been a hard last decade.
But I can fix this. It's my job to fix things.

Last month I heard a new joke
It's called Relationship OCD —
a new diagnosis. It's like an allergy
to intimacy, where the main symptom is fearing
how everyone else will be hurt by the allergy.

You probably haven't heard of it.
My shrink says it's trending in the literature,
but I was diagnosed before it got popular.
#PathologyHipster

Being funny is great though,
like being omniscient about a hypothetical
past where the punchline is the actual yesterday.
Dating is hard for me.

My last relationship
was eight panic attacks long.
Needless to say,
things got pretty serious.

Get it?
How when I sleep
next to someone who loves me
it's like the bed is crawling with spiders.

Get it? Like never having a family.
Wanting to be a father
but knowing I can never be
a partner. That's the joke.

I'm trying to get better.
I swear I can fix this.
Like a car.
Or a pet.

WHILE SCROLLING THROUGH HULU, AWAITING THE DELIVERY OF MY DOMINO'S THIN CRUST I CONSIDER THE HORRORS OF THE FREE MARKET

Child labor
Colonialism
Human trafficking

Global warming
Private prisons
Where is my pizza?

Economic collapse
For example, the Great Recession
Corporate cover-ups
For example, the ad said
my pizza would be here in 25 minutes
and it's been 28 minutes

Hunger
Famine
A knock at the door but it's just the wind
The telephone's blood-curdling scream
but it's not the pizza

I am starving
I am literally starving
I am Katniss Everdeen
but trapped by a paywall
I am the Donner party
but without their special pizza

Why do we accept this system built on the bending spine of labor
where *Die Hard* is no longer on streaming?

How can we live with an economy lubricated by blood
where I still don’t have my pizza?

What choice do I have but to continue my hunger strike?

COOKIE MONSTER HAS LEARNED A THING OR TWO ABOUT LATE-STAGE CAPITALISM SINCE SEASAME STREET MOVED TO PREMIUM CABLE

At old Sesame Street C was for Cookie!
At new Sesame Street

C STILL FOR COOKIE nom nom nom nom nom nom nom nom nom And Cookies still perfect because ALL COOKIES perfect!

But here, every cookie same type of perfect. Me don't know where Cookies come from. Me no heat oven. Me no put cookies on tray. Me no wear hat. They just sort of appear. Dressed in plastic. Perfect circles. Never crumble. Someone say "that's how the cookie crumbles." Me barely even remember what that means.

Sometimes me find me self forgetting how broken cookies can be perfect too or how crumbs form constellations on floor

But really me can't complain. Here, me no lift a finger but still have SO MANY COOKIES. Me open drawer — COOKIES! Me get in car — COOKIES! Me turn on computer — COOKIES! SUCH AN ABUNDANCE OF COOKIES! So much good nomming

even if made with cookie cutter. Though me worry new Sesame Street want Cookie Monster friends made with cookie cutter like Cookie Monster cookies. Maybe that why now Rowlf only play music that sound like elevator. Why Ernie and Bert no sleep in same room anymore. Why Oscar take bath (which actually me kind of ok with).

What next? Gonzo get nose job? Julia only appear at telethon? Miss Piggy use inside voice? Me concerned.

But luckily when me concerned me take solace in

COOKIES nom nom nom nom nom nom

then me feel better. Me no remember why me concerned in first place. Me just remember Cookies. Me just remember how much me love Cookies. Every Cookie. Every Cookie perfect.

REDACTION/ERASURE OF PRESIDENT BILL CLINTON'S SPEECH PROMOTING "WELFARE REFORM"

this is
the
cut/
the
sweeping
away/
make you work off
that
broken
chance/
that
tentative
shelter

we treat families with children the same
way we treat food
or
a mistake,
or
nothing

they face
America
alone

CLARENCE THOMAS AS RORSCHACH

It is probably not for me to speak on the racial hypocrisy

making his rank jurisprudence that much uglier, like a pubic hair
on a Coke can. After all, when, in my college years, I eagerly offered
my hot Caucasian takes on reparations, holistic admissions,
and history I was rightly called racist,

but never traitor.
My wide-eyed prejudice
seemed part of the natural order
and there was a strange forgiveness in that.
While Justice Thomas faces not only our condemnation
but also the double takes we afford him for seemingly
being a white supremacist
while Black.

As always, white people are unable to criticize a Black man
without taking aim at his Blackness. How I called him "an idiot"
and "the dumbest guy on the court"
before ever reading one of his opinions.
He isn't. In fact, he's probably the slyest
church snake in the pit. And doesn't the good judge
have the right to be called a

predatory nativist liar, billionaire tit suckling sycophant, Stop the Steal t-shirt mogul, transphobic aspiring nepo-grownup. Whiner. Asshole. Originalist. Tin foil hat matching power tie, so stuck in the past he still wears Rivers Cuomo glasses, J A N U A R Y 6 T H knuckle tatt, upside down flag, War on Christmas minuteman, Ginni's husband, integrity-starved Mel Gibson vicar

without another white person questioning whether
he is good enough at being Black?

GENTRIFIED CONTRAPUNTAL

I don't do my work
for my pocketbook

every new neighborhood

is its own reward.
But more than that
it's how when
my clients need me,

I know I will eventually
get to come running

without an escape route/
the slumlords
build up
a tower of ego/
a gentrified conscience

quietly, at the end of the way

back home

HOLY FUCKING SHIT! COMCAST HAS THE NUCLEAR LAUNCH CODES!

1.

On my seventh trip through the switchboard loop

I again press 9 to speak to a person

who sounds suspiciously like a robot

that only knows the phrase

how can I help you with that

to which I reply

I just want to talk to a person

which sounds suspiciously like

my internal monologue

when I'm not talking to Comcast.

2.

There are a lot of theories on how the world will end
but I think the most likely is that a nuclear strike
will be triggered by accident.

The President calls to stop it
only to face an impenetrable burg:

Thank you for accessing the Department of Defense Weapons of Mass Destruction Deployment System. If you are calling about nuclear weapons press 1. If you are calling about chemical or biological weapons press 2.

Please state or dial the Mk, TX, or B number of the missile you are calling about.

If you would like to go forward with the scheduled launch press 1. If you would like to delay the launch press 2. If the launch was triggered inadvertently press 3.

Thank you for accessing the Department of Defense Weapons of Mass Destruction Deployment System . . .

And as the President begs for live customer service,

the sky grows red.

The cockroaches conspire against any unlikely survivors.

3.

The distorted mind is a debt collector

calling at all hours.

Outstanding balance unknown.

Outstanding balance unknown.

Return to main menu.

I just want to talk to a person.

CHIEF JUSTICE ROBERTS VISITS AN INNER CITY SCHOOL ON A MOTIVATIONAL SPEAKING TOUR

Take responsibility.
A penny saved is a penny earned.
The only way to restore your right to vote is by voting.
If you don't have the time to both work
and care for your ailing mother
get a better job
or a healthier mother.

Build yourself up from nothing
like a universe colonizing the empty
like Christopher Columbus when he discovered
Pangea, lassoed our tectonic plate and drove it west.
Like I did. Like Jesus.
If he can then you can, too.
He was just a simple carpenter
who became the messiah.
And all he had to do
was die.

FROM THE PERSPECTIVE OF CHANUKAH

I am the American dream personified.
The essence of the self-made man.
Most people think I am the most important Jewish holiday.
I am not even in the Bible,
yet look at me alongside these others no one has heard of:
Shemini Atzeret. Simchat Torah. Tu B'Shvat.
When was the last time you saw a Yom Kippur Hallmark card?
Yom Kippur is about repentance and fasting.
Call it a High Holiday all you want,
but guilt and hunger don't sell.

I sell.

I started from the bottom.
Drake started a child star. I started with nothing. Yet here I am—
8 days of Xbox games, of slow dancing
with Geoffrey the Toys R Us giraffe.
I am so popular, Middle America Walmarts say *Happy Holidays*
on Christmas because of me, while I ride the season like a racehorse
yelling *location location location*
as Rosh Hashanah looks on longingly from autumn.
Sure, if I was a better man I might share the limelight
with these holier days devoted to family and forgiveness,
but this is capitalism. My value is in your hands,
and every year you choose me
against all odds.

I am not some feel-good Fourth of July:

> *Yay! We're free from England!*
> *We don't have to wear those fucking wigs anymore!*

My tale is one of right-wing Hebrews achieving victory
to better oppress moderate Jews.

But still, everyone loves me. I've got lunch boxes and shit.
I don't need that pansy-ass Thanksgiving's McGraw-Hill
textbook consultants to knit a quilt from my broken glass narrative.
I succeed, without help. I don't need help.

I was born on Christmas. Jesus wasn't even born on Christmas.

So take it from me, Jewish High Holidays,
with your three-hour liturgies
and introspective world peace bullshit.
What was your miracle, Pesach? Swarms of locusts? Stone tablets?
I'm sure those just fly off the shelf.
Oil was my miracle! That's that shit we go to war for.
Halliburton doesn't hire mercenaries to capture unleavened bread.
Your archaic rituals are fossils. I am the petroleum meniscus
rising above them.
Just watch my dreidel spin. Watch the winner
snatch up the pot. And why shouldn't he?

He earned it.

WEIRD, ZANY, AND HILARIOUS LAWS!

after Reader's Digest

In Connecticut, it is illegal to sell pickles that do not bounce

In Alaska, it is a crime to get drunk
at a bar

An ordinance in Gainesville, Georgia prohibits the consumption of fried chicken with utensils

Massachusetts forbids dancing to the National Anthem

In Minnesota, you may not grease
your
pig

Two Washington State counties fine residents for hunting Sasquatch

In Detroit, my client is losing her housing subsidy
because a friend
who showed up
uninvited
smoked weed
in her building
parking lot.

REDACTION/ERASURE OF PRESIDENT RONALD REAGAN'S 1985 STATE OF THE UNION ADDRESS

National security is government's first responsibility;
You know, we only have a military-industrial complex until a time of danger then it becomes the arsenal of
enterprise

Look to where peace and prosperity flourish today.
freedom is open

for
that dollar for dollar withdrawal

RONALD REAGAN WAS AN IDIOT (AND OTHER OBSERVATIONS ABOUT MY BIRTH YEAR)

I was born late.
I could give any number of reasons I wanted to stay put.
Every birth is a bad hair day for the baby. The star of *Bedtime for Bonzo*
had just been elected to lead us through the Cold War. Maybe I wanted
to stick it out until Christmas. Jews born on Christmas
wind up a pretty big deal sometimes.
Plus, the world can be a scary place. My mom
saw *The Shining* while I was in utero, though in my cocoon, it must
have sounded like a
            whisper wielding an axe.

There's nothing more sinister than a secret.
How it makes the ears twitch like a dog barking
at an earthquake that's not yet shook.
I wonder if I mouthed *Here's Johnny*
as I burst into the world.

I was born in the winter of 1981 to a twenty-below wind-chill.
In other words, I was born into a world where we still had winter.
They don't tell us their plans to poison the air
until the snow melts so the mosquitos can fly their violent love
            anywhere they wish.

When I was born, the president was an idiot.
Chalking this up to dementia
is an insult to dementia. But when you're born into the right skin
to parents who can tell the schools what to teach,
you can go from shitty actor to shitty governor to shitty president
and still die to become the deity so many pray to when they're laying
            awake at night fearing demographic shifts.

There's nothing more sinister than a secret
we all know but pretend to forget.
How every newborn is the property of their ancestors'

access to wheat. How the cradle
can be the grave. How the grave can be a magic phone booth
that makes men perfect,
            redacts our flaws like a designer toupee.

Every funeral is a good hair day for the dead. Even the most
desperate comb-over appears at peace. But the ice is thawing.
The seas are rising. And the warm, flooding earth
            doesn't preserve anything.

SUPREME COURT JUSTICE NEIL GORSUCH WILL NEVER FORGIVE THE EPA FOR THE DIVORSE OF HIS PARENTS

which took place in 1981 while his mother was serving as head of the Environmental Protection Agency after being appointed by President Ronald Regan

When the lonely begins to condense
in my throat
I dream back to 1980
when we were still a family
before the appointment
snatched the spatula
from Mother's hand
and sent her to Washington
leaving Daddy
to tend to so many feminine tasks —
a tired sobriety, the washing of laundry, a prudent erasure of tears
flowing down my cheeks like the rivers
Uncle Ronald made
her promise to never keep clean.

Once she took the post,
it was as if I wasn't her child anymore.
It was as if she had new children:
ExxonMobil DuPont Chemical.
So strict with me.
So lenient with them.

I'm not surprised
Mommy left Father
for Mr. Burford,
Chief of the *Bureau of Land Management.*
For who among us
can resist the raw sensuality
of government?

The rugged pheromones
of an administrative
cowboy?
The come hither stare
of a man delegated
so much power
to *manage land*?

But this, like many a tale that
begins with love,
ends with vengeance. With each bludgeon
of the gavel, another scar
heals. Each strike into EPA's cracking skull,
bellows from the bench:
"This is for Daddy. And this is for me.
And this is for children everywhere
torn from their mother's teat
by the Hydra of the regulatory state."

As I have always said, revenge is a dish best served cold
as a frozen trucker fleeing
the Department of Labor's suffocating blanket.
It took Andronicus, Dantès, Montoya
a lifetime to exact reprisal.
And that's exactly how long I have.

CAPITALISM or THE ART OF THE ACTUARY or REAL PIMPS
GET PAID IN PREMIUMS or AUTOMATIC WITHDRAWAL: A
TALE OF TWO KIDNEYS or CHOKING IS LIKE FIRST BASE
TO ADAM SMITH'S INVISIBLE HANDS or SOPHIE'S
CHOICE ULTIMATUM: RENT OR INSULIN or HAVING
TO EXPLAIN TO A STRANGER WHY I NEED PROZAC
TO GET COVERAGE FOR PROZAC IS THE KIND
OF SHIT THAT MAKES ME NEED PROZAC or
DIRTY HARRY VI: YOU ONLY GET GOOD
NEWS FROM YOUR LIFE INSURANCE
COMPANY WHEN YOU'RE DEAD or
9 TO 5 TO 9 TO 5 TO 9 TO 5
TO 9 TO 5 TO 9 TO 5 TO 9
TO 5 TO 9 TO 5 TO 9
TO 5 TO 9 TO 5
TO 9 TO 5 TO
9 TO 5...

As your attorney,
I must advise you
that acquiescing
to liquidation
is probably
your most
cost-effective
option.

ODE [DIS TRACK] TO MY STAPLE REMOVER

Prehistoric fangs/ hungry metal teeth beast/ crawled to land sea creature/ eager cleaver/ bites the hand that feeds/ But these days it's an accident/ been settling for scraps since/ you got cornered to a drawer/ and sent to bed without a sacrament/ Domesticated/ it's depressing/ blue pill glutton/ peaceful Patty Hearst/ rendered useless/ vestigial tool/ compared to hands you do the same tasks worse/ So what's your purpose?/ What's your worth? You're just/ a head beneath the mantel/ just a predator turned scavenger/ barely an animal/ castrated cannibal/ emasculated mandible/ man-made man's aid makes the Gilded Age laughable/ You've become another joke/ You choke/ but barely make the paper rip/ Once were saber-tipped/ Now you're only spayed and limp/ Your bite is like a hunter/ teeth-bore/ throat open/ ancient fish/ but just what do I need you for that I can't do with a paperclip?

TRANSCRIPT OF THE CHICK-FIL-A COW MASCOT'S TESTIMONY BEFORE A WAR CRIME TRIBUNAL

Mascot :

Moo. Moo. Moo. Moo. Moo.

Translation:

On the farm, I would wake up to the rooster's crow until I grew so accustomed I started sleeping right through it. It's kind of like that. After a while, the screams just sounded like morning. Like another day at work.

I wanted to be good at my job. I played the part. Waved the "eat more chicken" sign like it could just as easily be a rooster out front and me on the grill.

I adopted the proper language, straight from the manual. We weren't "priming a killing machine," just "boiling water." We weren't "filleting my friends," just "making a sandwich." That wasn't my old buddy Sergeant Feathers or Madame Clucks-A-Lot. Just Order Number 5. Order Number 6. Number 7. Number 8. Number 9.

We were just following orders.

Number 1. Number 2. Number 3. Number 4.

Number 4 with cheese. Number 5
with bacon. Bacon. Not pig. Not Peppa, Porky,

Piggins, Piggie Smalls, Spammy Kolfax, or John Ham.[1] Not the skin and fat and muscle of something that once had a name.

---

1 *See also, e.g.*, Porkey, Hogwarts, Piggins, Sir Oinks-a-Lot, Elvis Pigsley, Madame Porksworth, Albert Oinkstein, Curly, Snorts, Tootsie, Tidy Tim, Jean Paul Snout, MC Hammer.

THE AUTHOR TRIES TO WRITE A LOVE POEM/ THE GOLEM WRITES A LOVE POEM

It's not that I want to fuck you
It's more that I want to fuck
Up anyone who's ever done you wrong
Not so much because you need protecting
But more because I need a jaw to store
My fists in

It's not that I love you
It's more that I hate everyone
Who doesn't
And anger is all I know
Or maybe it's just done more
Good than my love has
The love always ends in an eviction
But the anger doesn't leave me
It breathes me awake every morning, says

GO TO WORK
GO TO COURT
DEFEND A STRANGER
GO SOMEWHERE
OTHER THAN WHEREVER YOU ARE
RIGHT NOW
A PARTICLE IS NEVER STILL
AND YOU ARE JUST A BILLION
ANGRY PARTICLES
QUIVERING FOR THE LOVE YOU NEVER FOUND
ALL SHAKE NO SHIMMY
ALL TEETH NO BONE
ALL ANGER AND THE ABSENCE OF LOVE AND THE LOVE
OF THAT ANGER THAT EMULSIFIES UNTIL THAT IS ALL YOU ARE

And that is all I am now
A shark
Trying to unlearn
Its own mouth
Or learn back yours
Or just remember
Today
That I'm hungry
And I'm parched for blood
But only that of those
Who force you to summon the mud

FOR THE POETS WHO APOLOGIZE FROM THE MICROPHONE

They say talk is cheap, but really
words are a currency of unpredictable value.

Jesus of Nazareth says
we must feed and clothe the poor
and gives up his life to do so.

Joseph Stalin says
we must feed and clothe the poor
and kills millions of Soviets to do so,
banishes millions more to Siberia.
If only he'd been less invested
in his words.

A room is only as secure as the lock on the door.

A poet thanks the host for providing a safe space
and tells a tale of deeply personal trauma.
They are applauded for their honesty and vulnerability.

A poet thanks the host for providing a safe space
and performs a piece stating that in retrospect
he should have realized she said "no."
He is applauded for his honesty and vulnerability.
Even after complaints, the host refuses to exclude him from events.

Says *this must be a safe space for everyone.*
Says *restorative justice and presumption of innocence*
and *forgiveness.*
Pretends pacifism is more than voyeurism waving a flag.
Says *how can we punish anyone for speaking their truth?*

So then how strong of a currency is truth?
Is it tied to the dollar? The euro?
Is it a safer investment than, say, a war bond?
Do we prop its value by creating artificial scarcity
until the market grows bullish?

Maybe it isn't talk that's cheap.
Maybe it's safety.

After all, every space is safe
for someone.

Sure, the needle may puncture the vein
but isn't the vein the safest space for the needle?

Sure, we should save the Siberian tiger
but doesn't that seal the fate of its prey?

Linguists once believed meaning
derived from the intent of the speaker.
Now they believe it derives from the perception of the listener.
Which means that my ruminations are meaningless —
the obsessions, just an echo,
words tied to nothing.

The poet calls himself an ally now.
Says he is so sorry.
That must be worth
something.

REDACTION/ERASURE OF BRETT KAVANAUGH'S TESTIMONY TO THE SENATE

Mr. Chairman, I wrote myself an equivocal
recollection,
something, anything to
block the
evil. nightmare of
meaning.

listen carefully. To my family,
consequence is
violence.

You may defeat me but never
the revenge, the barrier,
the refuted
onslaught of time.

That's who I am.
America.
a good
Holy brutal
church.

We
always had a lot of
women and beer.

I liked beer. I still like beer. I drink beer to black out an ugly

vilified

yesterday

with

the light of God.

I'll be the first justice in the history of the Supreme Court to have women

I respect.

I revere

President Trump for

Explaining this to our daughters.

BLOOD MOON

I did not make it out to see the blood moon, but I hear it was a once-in-a-lifetime kind of beautiful. The kind of beauty that birthed the first prayer. The kind you just want to stare at for as long as you can though it doesn't much change except maybe if an airplane flies across it which is beautiful too and also a metaphor for childlike wonder or the allure of a colonized sky and what could be more beautiful than an endless sky all our own? But maybe   I don't care

about beauty. Maybe I just want to tattoo records to my hard drive and think about ugly things: boarded homes or suburban sprawl or that bursting capillary in my left eye in the second grade when I stood up to a bully for the first time. How a red hue crept across my cornea and for a whole month every moon was tinted plasma. Maybe I just want to lie here until I'm done dreaming of nothing and morning rustles my hair and tells me to know this day fearlessly despite the inevitability of everyone talking about the blood moon. How it reached through the sky like a prophecy and made everything beautiful: the sunsets rising from smokestacks, the ocean-blue eyes of billboards. How its   blood

red bloom lent a glint of lavender to the flag-draped casket of a fallen man pronounced hero. How the tombstones were transformed to ruby. How the bereaved found God in its glow. How the autumn grass surrounding the grave was just the right amount of   dead.

CONTRAPUNTAL FOR EVICTION AND HOPE

<table>
<tr><td>there is no goodbye/</td><td>there is just broken credit/</td></tr>
<tr><td>just leaving/</td><td>the payday loan scavengers
licking their chops/</td></tr>
<tr><td>you’ll never see</td><td>the recovery, a snail wandering</td></tr>
<tr><td>the neighborhood</td><td>desperate for progress/</td></tr>
<tr><td>grieving/
never find a way to</td><td>but you’ll
give up/
you don’t need to</td></tr>
<tr><td>bring anything with you/</td><td>try to remember</td></tr>
<tr><td>you can only leave</td><td>how it was once</td></tr>
<tr><td></td><td>before you’re
headed somewhere new/</td></tr>
<tr><td>an empty house of
empty rooms/</td><td></td></tr>
<tr><td></td><td>you’ll feel how love
is more than</td></tr>
<tr><td>just fixtures
and walls/</td><td>you can bear to leave</td></tr>
<tr><td>the skeletons —</td><td>hope is</td></tr>
<tr><td>a still
living family</td><td></td></tr>
</table>

moving away.

EXODUS

> "You shall no longer give the people straw to make bricks... let them go and gather straw for themselves."
>
> — Exodus 5:6

and then the rental subsidies all dried up like so much once-tillable land, the type where no one can live now, not even plants, not unless your strange and vengeful god places you there to wander for forty years so you spend the next four millennia thanking him anyway because at least it's better than Egyptian chains.

and then across an ocean, how the bottom dropped out from under the economy like a breaking bridge and there was nothing left to build with and we daily mourned how homeownership became a deadweight tied to the drowning American dream while rarely mentioning so many who paid to live on another's land now banished to the desert, but this time they hadn't prayed for freedom from Pharaoh, just to stay in one place, keep their kids in the same school district,

to exist. After all, *I think therefore I am* doesn't mean much outside the classroom. In the rest of the world, you've gotta have an address. As it is written:

On the 1st day,

god said *let there be light*
but the next month it
was shut off for nonpayment

On the 3rd day,
god made land

On the 6th day,
god said this land

would be owned and
those without a
plot to their name
would thereafter wander
through the desert to Jerusalem
or from their bed to their friend's couch
to the street to their mom's couch
to the street again until they find a pasture
whose master grants them entry
though the Lord will still own their yield

and then the manna in heaven all dried up when we embraced his most mysterious ways and insisted on employment requirements and drug tests for food stamps, Medicaid, TANF. So you have to work to prove you're too sick to work. So you have to pay rent to get help paying rent. Plus, for god to even acknowledge your prayers at all, you've gotta have an address.

button poetry

ACKNOWLEDGEMENTS

Eric would first like to thank his wonderful wife Emma for her encouragement, insight, and for being cute. He is also extremely grateful to his Mom, Dad, sister Sara, brother-in-law Aaron and his wee nieces Kira and Ellie. Eric would also like to express tremendous gratitude to all of the people who helped edit and improve this book: Button Poetry (especially Tanesha Kozler, Audrey Hoisington, and Charley Eatchel!) Adrienne Nadeau, Mojdeh Stoakley, Lannie Stabile, Jason B. Crawford, and many others which are arbitrarily escaping Eric's mind but who he will feel bad about not thanking later.

"When a real adult walks into my office seeking legal advice"
was published by *The Portland Review*

"It's my job to fix things" was published as
"I am funny" by *Voicemail Poems*

"[They] Don't Really Care If You Cry"
was published by *The Daily Drunk*

"Blood Moon" was published by
Meow Meow Pow Pow Lit

"The Foreclosure Crisis, Explained through the First 80 Minutes of Disney's *The Lion King*" and "From the Perspective of Chanukah"
were published by *FreezeRay Poetry* ("...Chanukah" was also published by Wild Pressed Books)

"Ronald Reagan was an idiot" was published by
Entropy, Alternating Currents, and Wild Pressed Books

"For the poets who apologize from the microphone" was inspired by "Written to be Yelled at Trump Tower During a Vigil for The NEA" by sam sax

ABOUT THE AUTHOR

Eric Sirota is a poet and lawyer living in Chicago. By day, Eric is an attorney who has spent his career advocating for low-income tenants and homeowners in a variety of contexts. Currently, Eric directs the Tenant Advocacy Clinic at Northwestern Pritzker School of Law. Previously, he worked as the Director of Housing Justice at the Shriver Center on Poverty Law. Eric has also worked for Legal Aid, at law school clinics providing legal services to veterans and representing borrowers in foreclosure, and in the Illinois Attorney General's Consumer Protection Bureau. By night, Eric does artsy stuff. His chapbooks have been published by Wild Pressed Books and *FreezeRay Poetry*. He is a two-time Chicago venue Grand Slam Champion and a Best-of-the-Net nominated artist. Eric releases deeply neurotic hip hop under the moniker Rota, a nickname he was given by friends in 6th grade to distinguish him from another Eric. You can't miss him. He's the tallest Jew for miles.

AUTHOR BOOK RECOMMENDATIONS

If My Body Could Speak by Blythe Baird

Blythe Baird's writing is so empathetic that her personal feels universal and her universal feels personal, even when she is recalling an experience I cannot relate to in any immediate sense. Baird has a remarkable ability to express her reality, her inner life, her interrogation of her inner life, and her interrogation of her interrogation of her inner life with a seemingly impossible balance of nuance and relatability. We read her book, and even if we are middle-aged, and even if the imagery of her childhood does not match ours, we find ourselves both oddly nostalgic for and relieved to have moved past our younger years, though with lingering doubt that we truly have or ever will. I re-read Baird's deservedly acclaimed "Girl Code 101" and am called to both urgent introspection and indignation, though I have been out of high school for 24 years. I'm reminded how the lifelong process of pain, healing, and growth began in earnest when I first tried to name it, but also how that naming can itself be confining and complex. Baird shies away from none of this. To say there is 'something for everyone' in *If My Body Could Speak* is to give it too little credit. Rather, the work is a Rorschach on both childhood and adulthood that should scare and soothe all of us.

The Crown Ain't Worth Much by Hanif Abdurraqib

I don't know a single author who would not enter into a Faustian bargain to write like Hanif. He embraces contradictions — colloquialism and refinement, grief and joy, music and silence — with such profound expertise that they stop being contradictions at all. Rather, they are all just tools in Hanif's seemingly unending literary toolbox. I'm fully convinced Hanif could write a poem about paint drying, grass growing, a carton of milk, and somehow make it both transcendent and profoundly grounded in a specific location, timeless and anchored to a specific moment in his life — both vulnerable confession and brilliant sociological microcosm. Maybe those are the ingredients of the best prayers. Or the best jokes. Or the best conversations with old friends and passing strangers alike. When Hanif writes a poem like "In Defense of the Word 'Moist'" it almost seems like he is doing so on a dare to prove that he can. And he always can, in ways no reader could ever expect. We are lucky to be contemporaries with someone who can write like this. His entry points into any subject feel both wholly surprising and inevitable. Every word feels like the best reveal.

Autopsy by Donte Collins

I found myself laughing quite a bit while reading Donte Collins' brilliant collection *Autopsy*. This may be an unexpected reaction, but I don't think it should be. First, while the book is quite a ways from 'comedy,' Collins has an undeniably sly and brutal sense of humor, which extracts the humor from tragedy and vice versa ("my deepest condolences: if you died I would make a Facebook status"). In other words, often I laugh because Donte is funny — in the best possible way. At other times, I found myself laughing the way one does when a close friend breaks a hard truth to you with perfectly precise language, as if revealing something you already knew but hoped you were wrong about ("sometimes I feel earth becoming motherless"). Other times, it is just hard not to chuckle in disbelief over Collins' pure talent and artistry, as if to say 'how did they do that?' or 'how did they know how to say that like that?' ("do you still perform autopsies on conversations you've had lives ago?"; "she's been gone 15,840 minutes & you have felt the godless storm of each of them") Gah! Tragedy and comedy have always been strange yet persistent bedfellows and Collins engages with the former so perfectly that it can't help but cuddle up a bit with the latter.

OTHER BOOKS BY BUTTON POETRY

If you enjoyed this book, please consider checking out some of our others, below. Readers like you allow us to keep broadcasting and publishing. Thank you!

Omar Holmon, *We Were All Someone Else Yesterday*
Rachel Wiley, *Fat Girl Finishing School*
Bianca Phipps, *crown noble*
Natasha T. Miller, *Butcher*
Kevin Kantor, *Please Come Off-Book*
Ollie Schminkey, *Dead Dad Jokes*
Reagan Myers, *Afterwards*
L.E. Bowman, *What I Learned From the Trees*
Patrick Roche, *A Socially Acceptable Breakdown*
Rachel Wiley, *Revenge Body*
Ebony Stewart, *BloodFresh*
Ebony Stewart, *Home.Girl.Hood.*
Kyle Tran Myhre, *Not A Lot of Reasons to Sing, but Enough*
Steven Willis, *A Peculiar People*
Topaz Winters, *So, Stranger*
Darius Simpson, *Never Catch Me*
Blythe Baird, *Sweet, Young, & Worried*
Siaara Freeman, *Urbanshee*
Robert Wood Lynn, *How to Maintain Eye Contact*
Junious 'Jay' Ward, *Composition*
Usman Hameedi, *Staying Right Here*
Sean Patrick Mulroy, *Hated for the Gods*
Sierra DeMulder, *Ephemera*
Taylor Mali, *Poetry By Chance*
Matt Coonan, *Toy Gun*
Matt Mason, *Rock Stars*
Miya Coleman, *Cottonmouth*
Ty Chapman, *Tartarus*
Lara Coley, *ex traction*
DeShara Suggs-Joe, *If My Flowers Bloom*
Ollie Schminkey, *Where I Dry the Flowers*
Edythe Rodriguez, *We, the Spirits*
Topaz Winters, *Portrait of My Body as a Crime I'm Still Committing*
Zach Goldberg, *I'd Rather Be Destroyed*

Available at buttonpoetry.com/shop and more!